WILLIAM BOLCOM

FRESCOES

War In Heaven
The Caves of Orcus

for
TWO KEYBOARD PLAYERS
at
TWO PIANOS, HARMONIUM, HARPSICHORD

As recorded on Naxos 8.559244

Two copies necessary for performance

EDWARD B. MARKS MUSIC COMPANY

EXCLUSIVELY DISTRIBUTED BY
HAL•LEONARD® CORPORATION
7777 W. BLUEMOUND RD. P.O. BOX 13819 MILWAUKEE, WI 53213

Printed in U.S.A.

FRESCOES
I. War In Heaven

WILLIAM BOLCOM

Presto furioso THUNDEROUS

as fast as possible

Piano I

Piano II

I

II

*For performance notes, please see page 32.

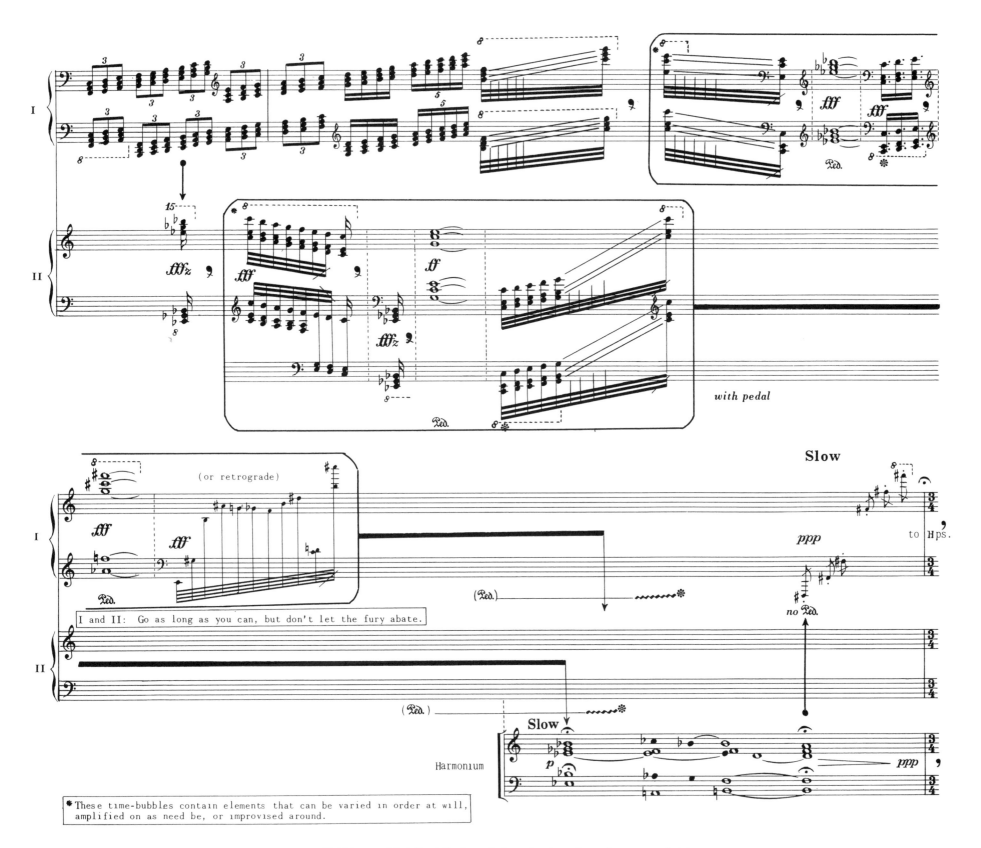

(or retrograde)

with pedal

Slow

to Hps.

I and II: Go as long as you can, but don't let the fury abate.

(Ped.)

no Ped.

Slow

Harmonium

✻These time-bubbles contain elements that can be varied in order at will, amplified on as need be, or improvised around.

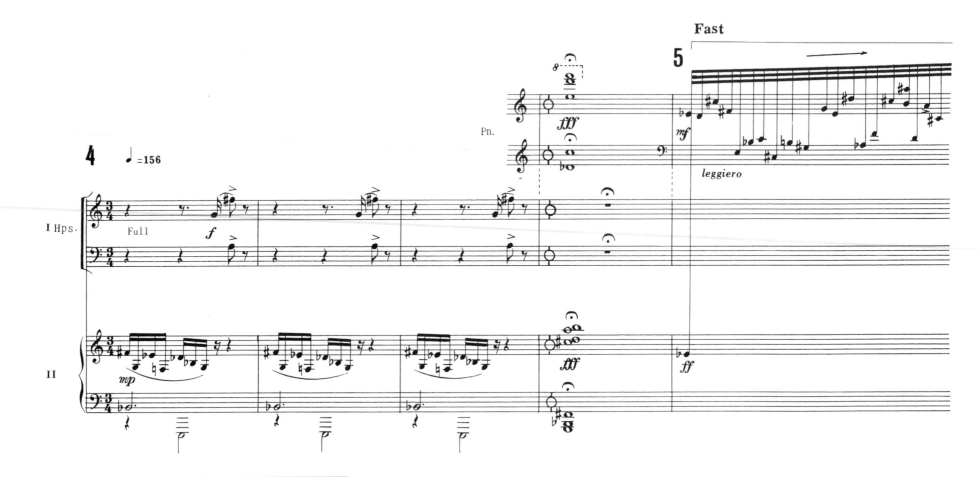

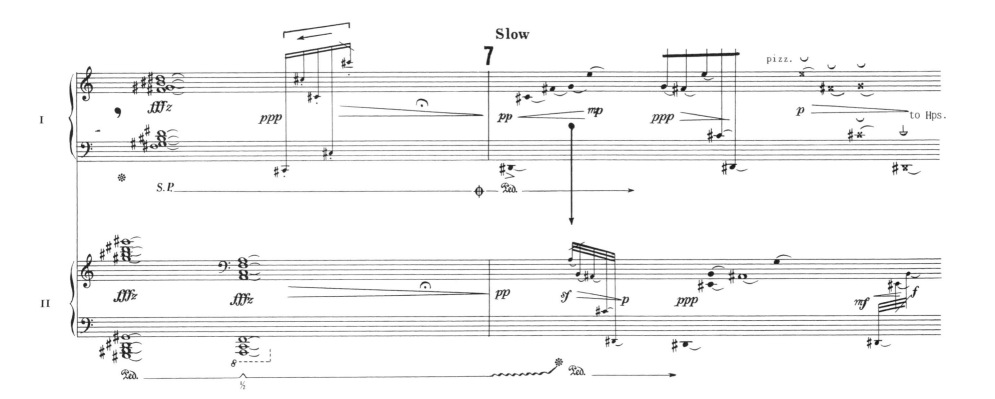

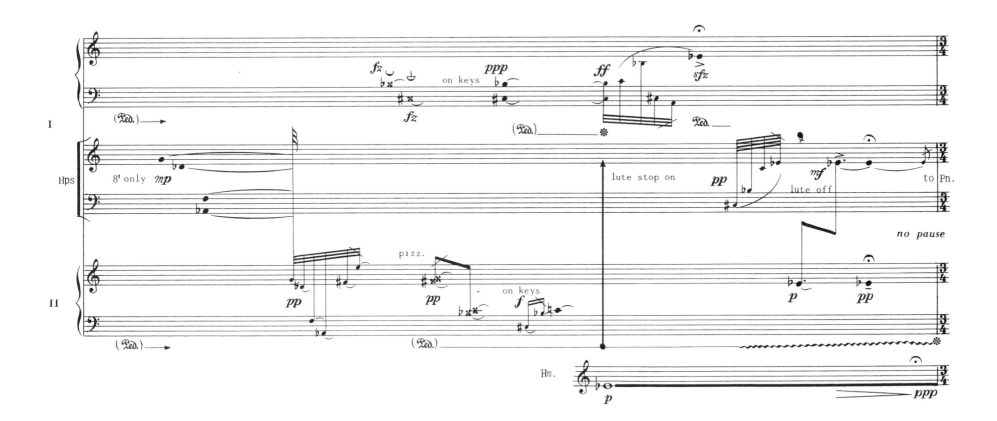

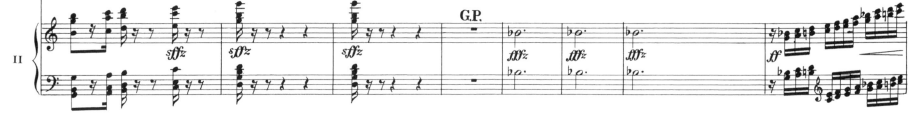

♩ = 54 ←→ 72

8' 16' only

I Hps.

mf

even;"quasi legato"

(non-synchronized with Hps.)

II Hm.

mp

steady

I

II

steady

17

I

II

✸ No rhythmic structure; the 16ths are separated for ease of reading.

18

steady   8' lute stop✻   16' lute stop

✻ Add lute stops as you can, depending on the harpsichord.

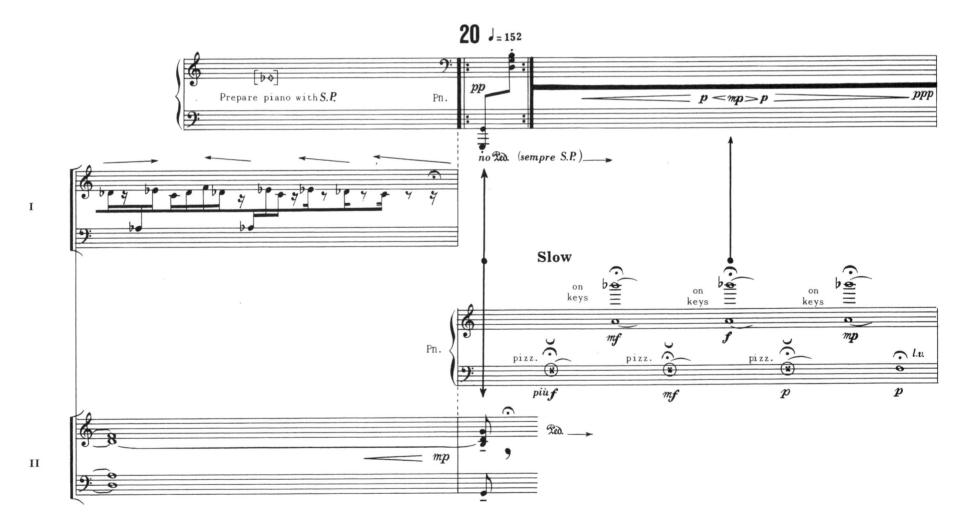

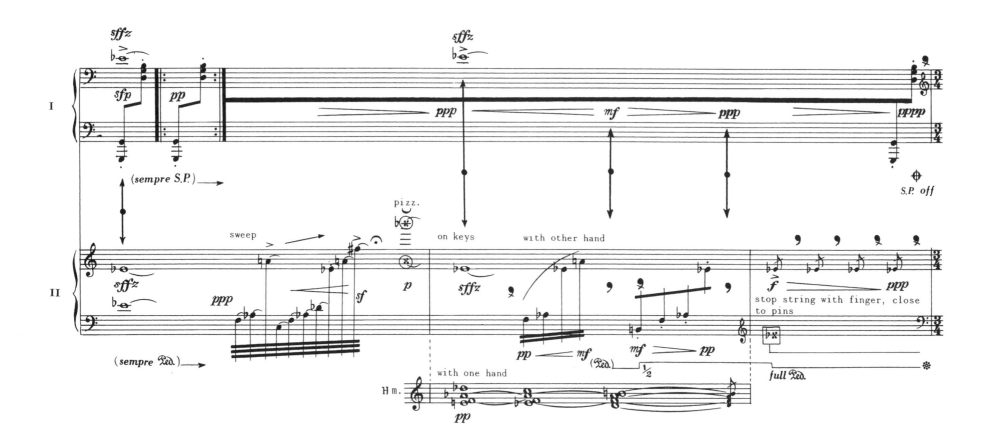

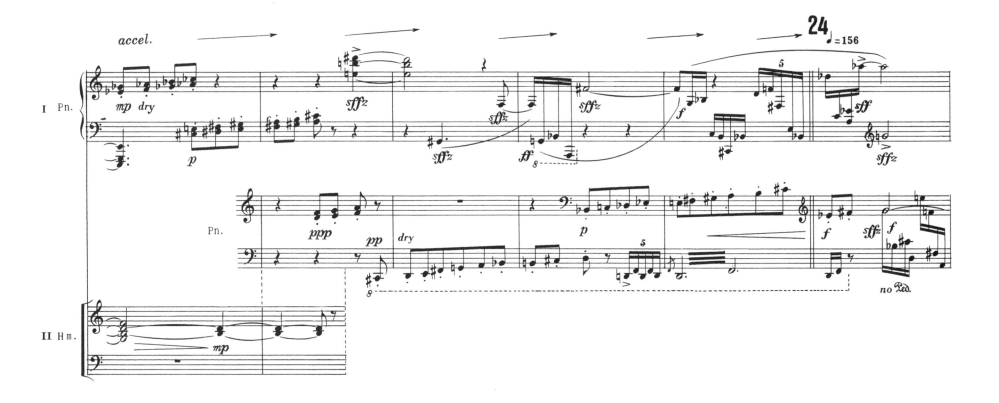

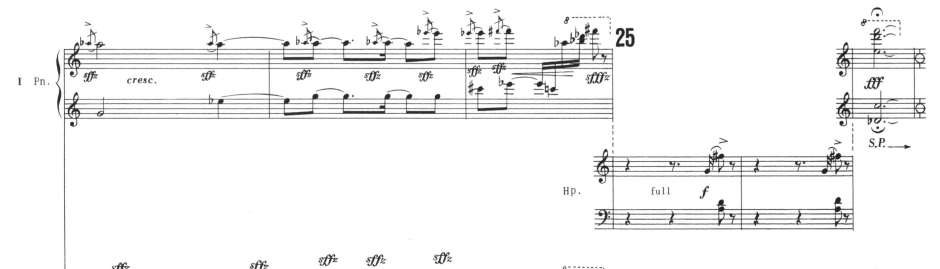

Tug of War ("*pull*" *at each other*)

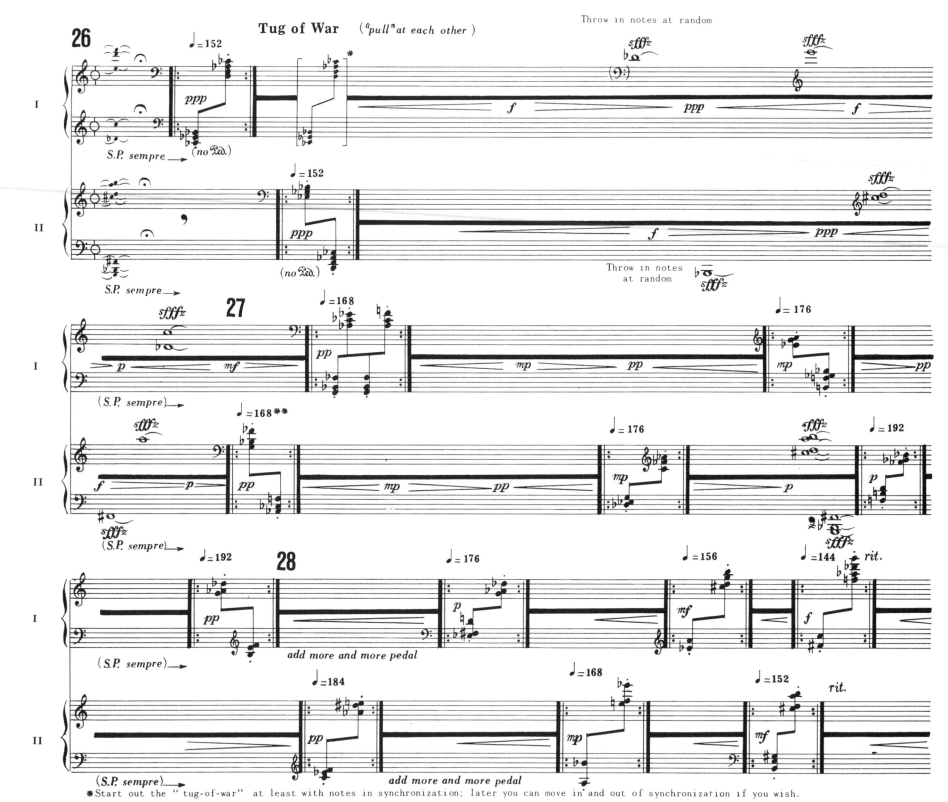

Throw in notes at random

*Start out the " tug-of-war " at least with notes in synchronization; later you can move in and out of synchronization if you wish.

**It is not so important that these markings be metronomically exact as that they should be <u>relative</u> to each other.

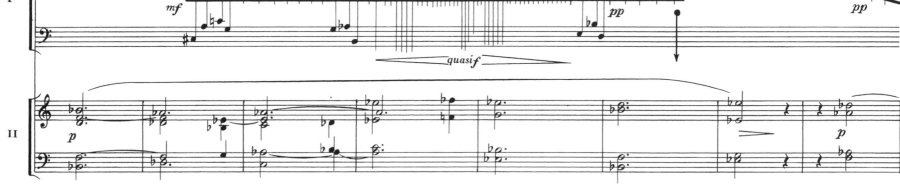

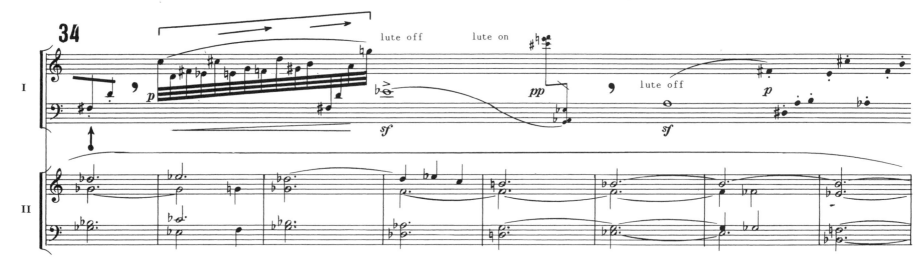

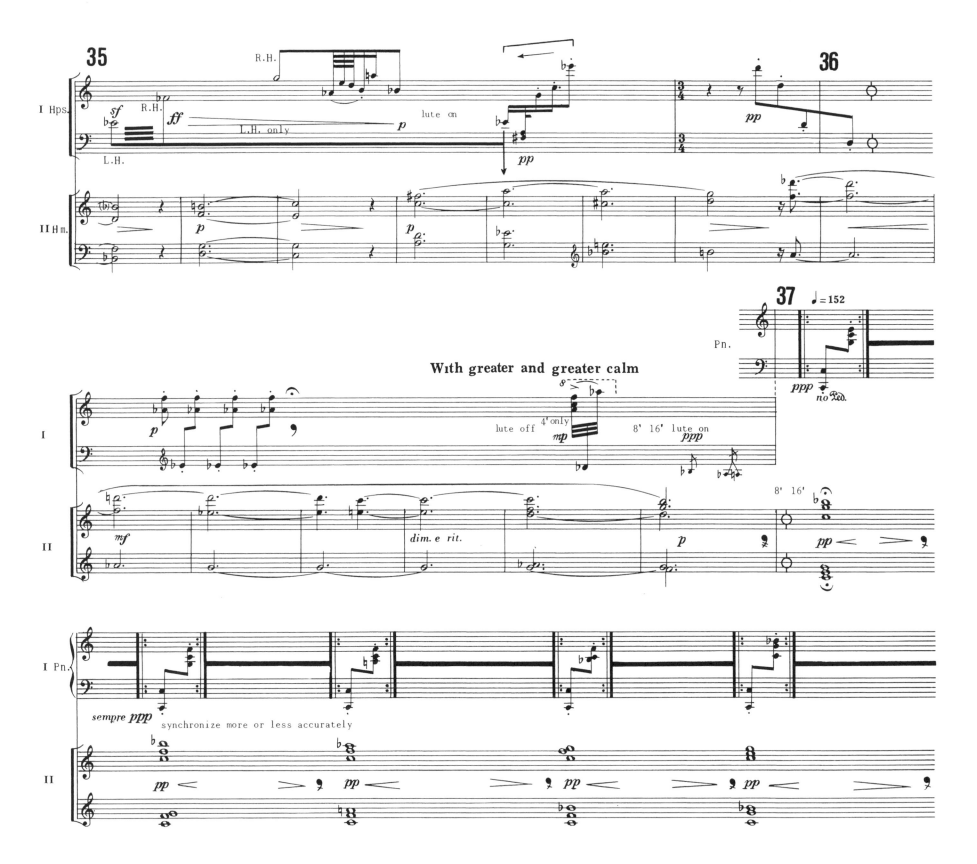

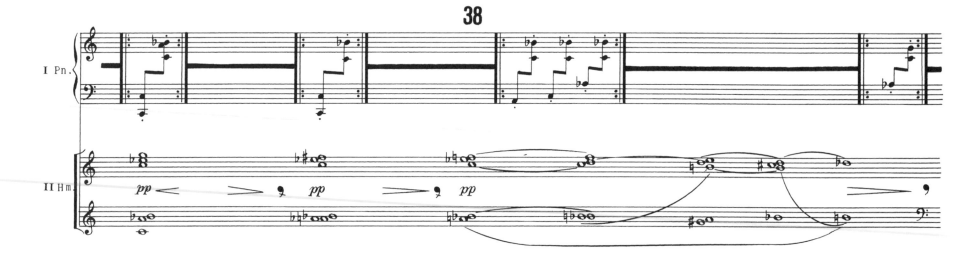

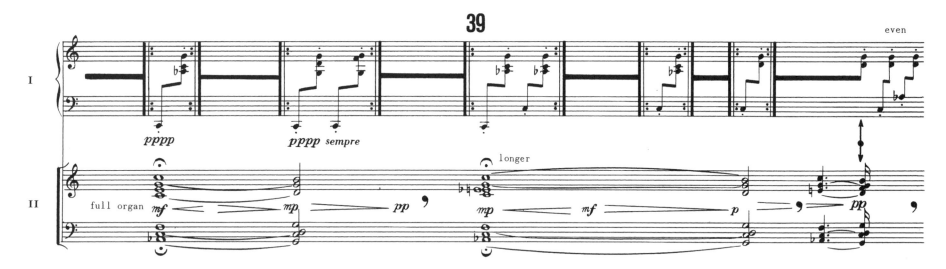

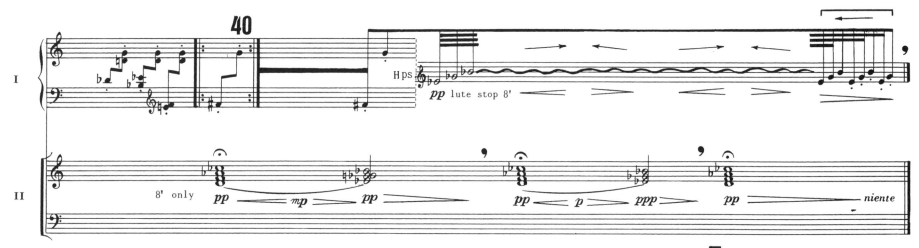

WAIT 5", then follow with the next movement

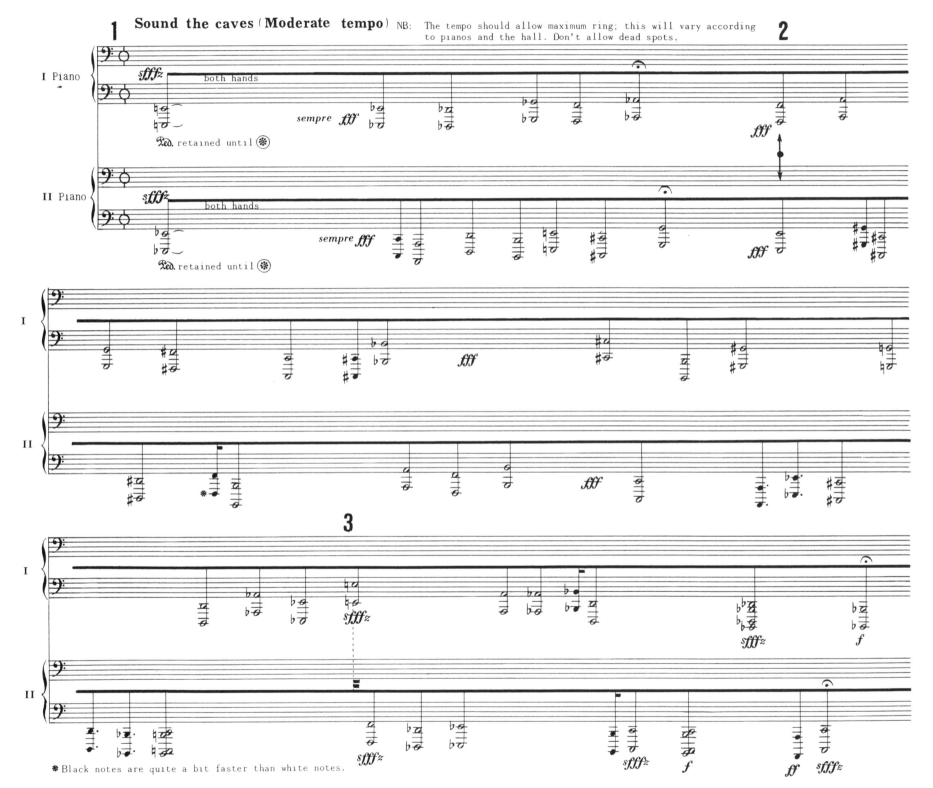

* Black notes are quite a bit faster than white notes.

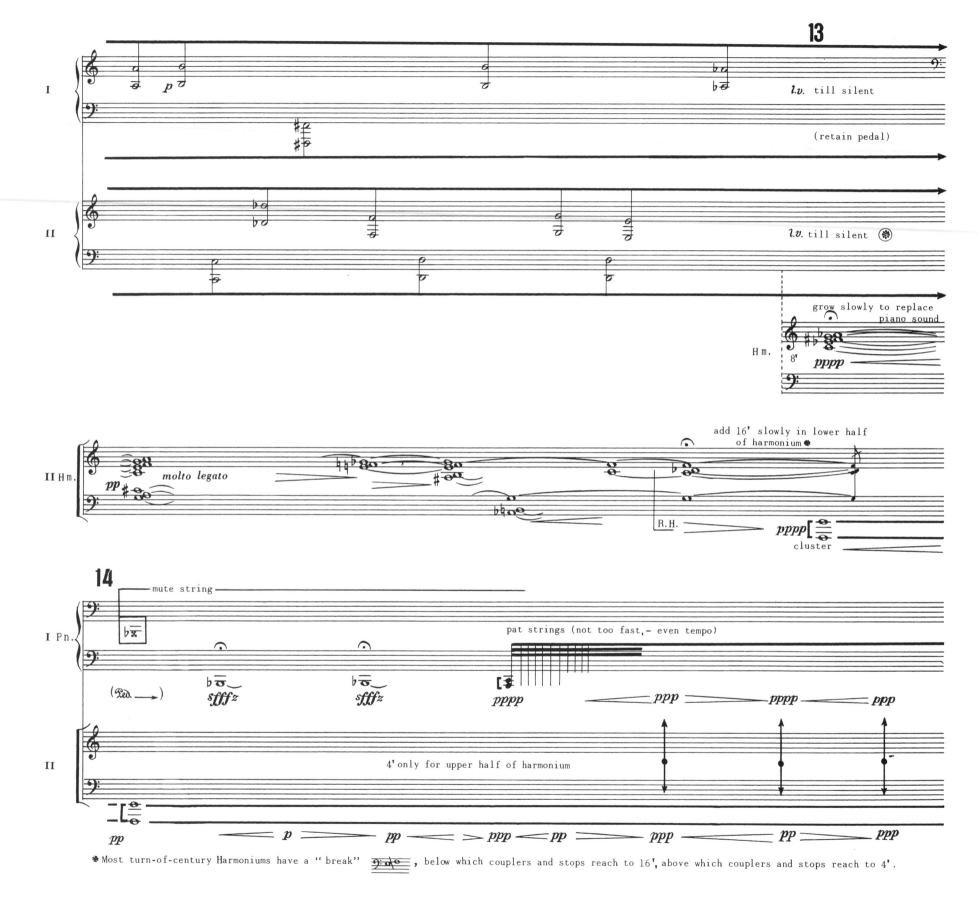

13

I

l.v. till silent

(retain pedal)

II

l.v. till silent ✸

grow slowly to replace
piano sound

Hm.   8'   *pppp*

add 16' slowly in lower half
of harmonium ✸

II Hm.   *molto legato*

pp

R.H.   *pppp* [
cluster

14

mute string

I Pn.

pat strings (not too fast, – even tempo)

(Ped. ⟶)   *sfffz*   *sfffz*   *pppp*   *ppp*   *pppp*   *ppp*

II

4' only for upper half of harmonium

pp   *p*   *pp*   *ppp*   *pp*   *ppp*   *pp*   *ppp*

✸ Most turn-of-century Harmoniums have a " break " , below which couplers and stops reach to 16', above which couplers and stops reach to 4'.

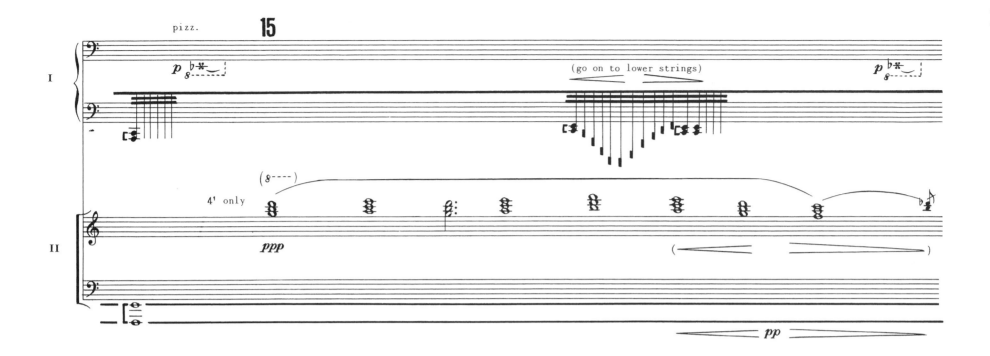

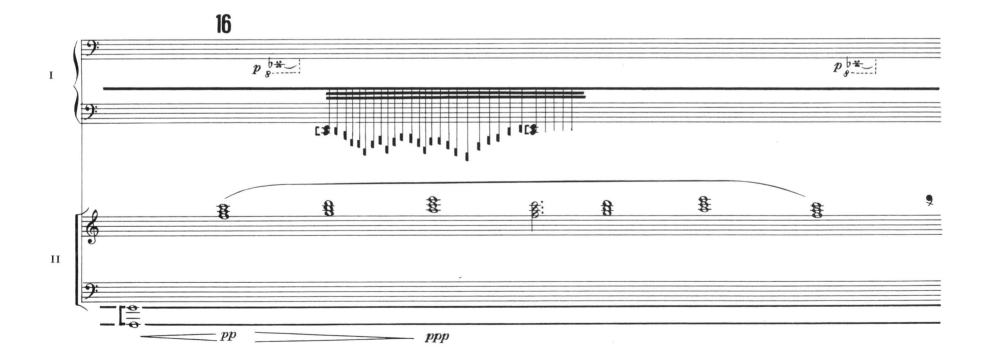

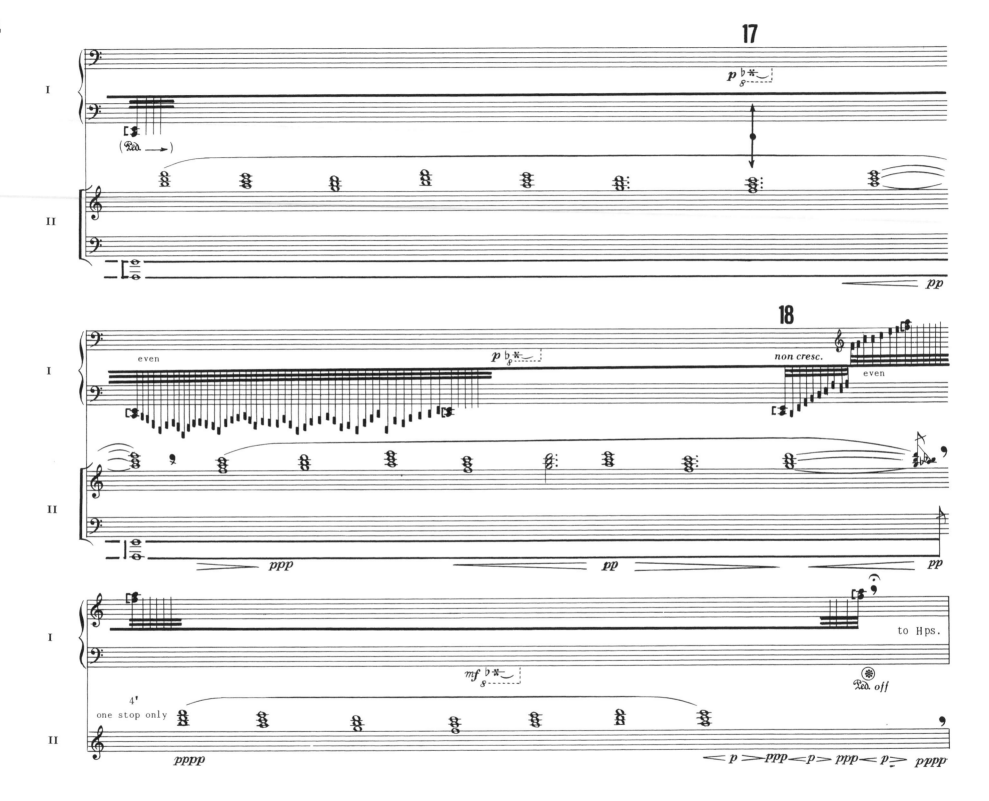

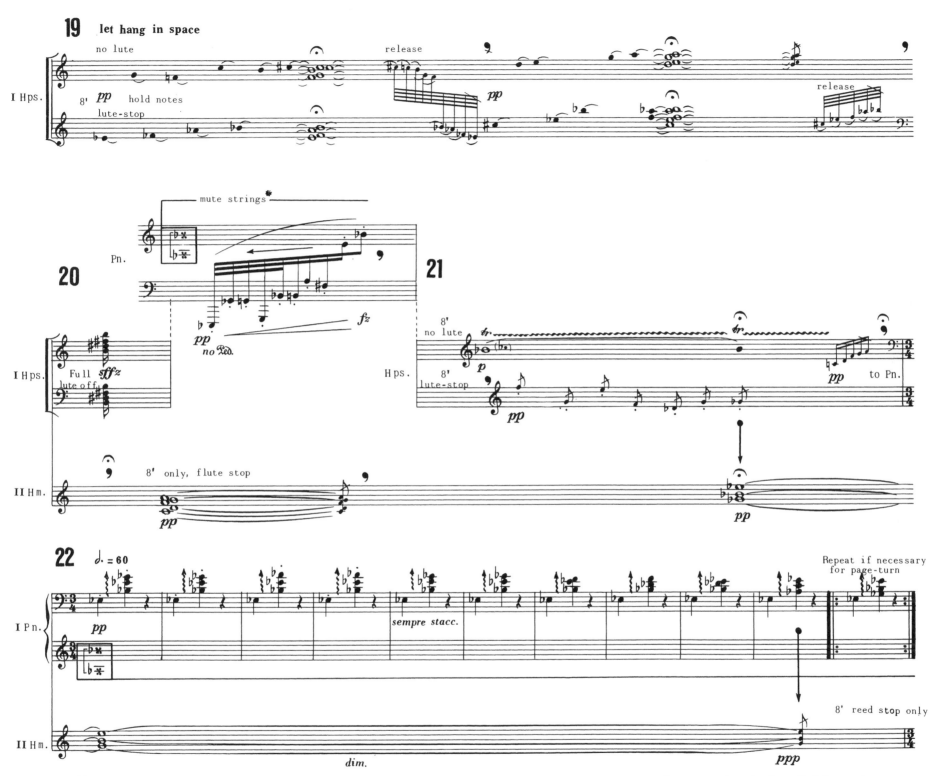

*To mute these strings, place an object such as a large, full coin-purse (for the weight) on the strings, at least covering the described interval, but not covering ⟪notation⟫ The weight should be placed just behind the dampers.

Dance of the Denizens of Death

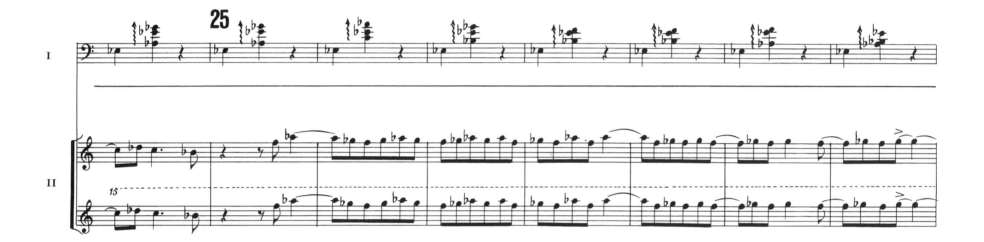

Repeat if necessary

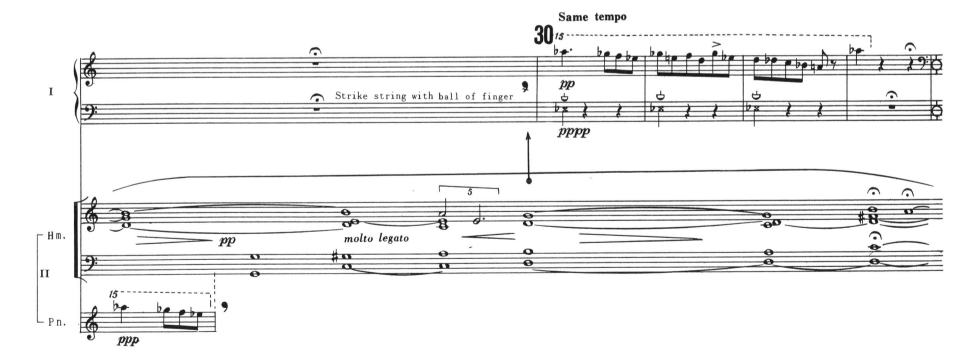

31 **Extremely slow**

Lowest keys; like a blast in the center of the earth

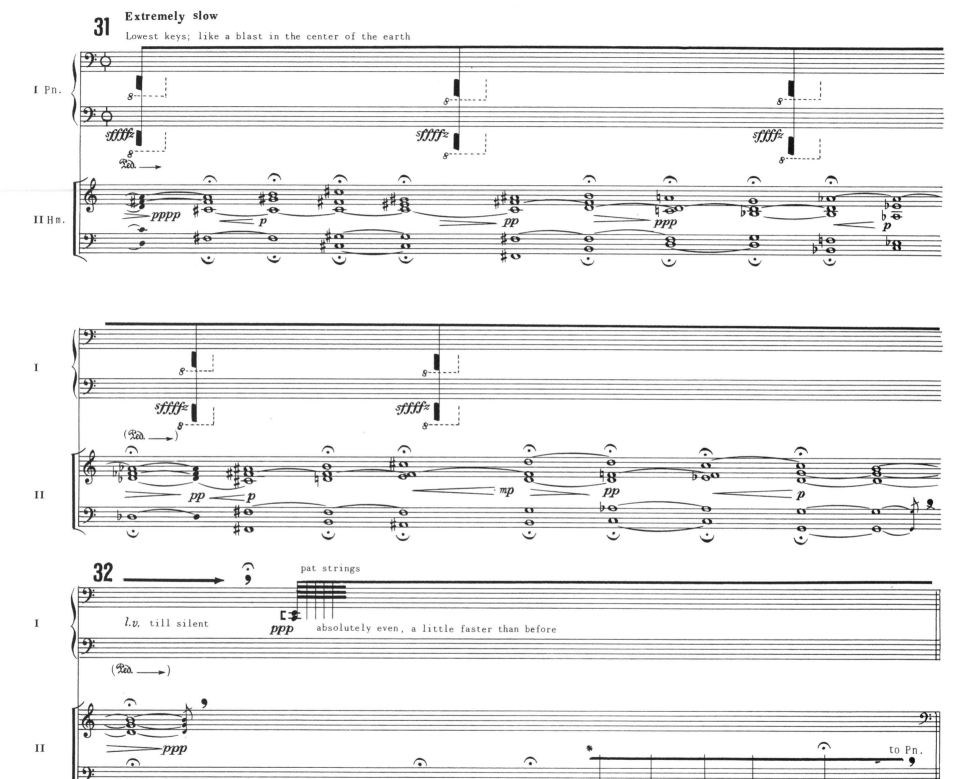

pat strings

l.v. till silent

ppp absolutely even, a little faster than before

to Pn.

G♭ ppp < pp > ppp < pp > ppp niente
F pp > ppp < pp > ppp

＊This is done by alternating relative pressure on the two keys.

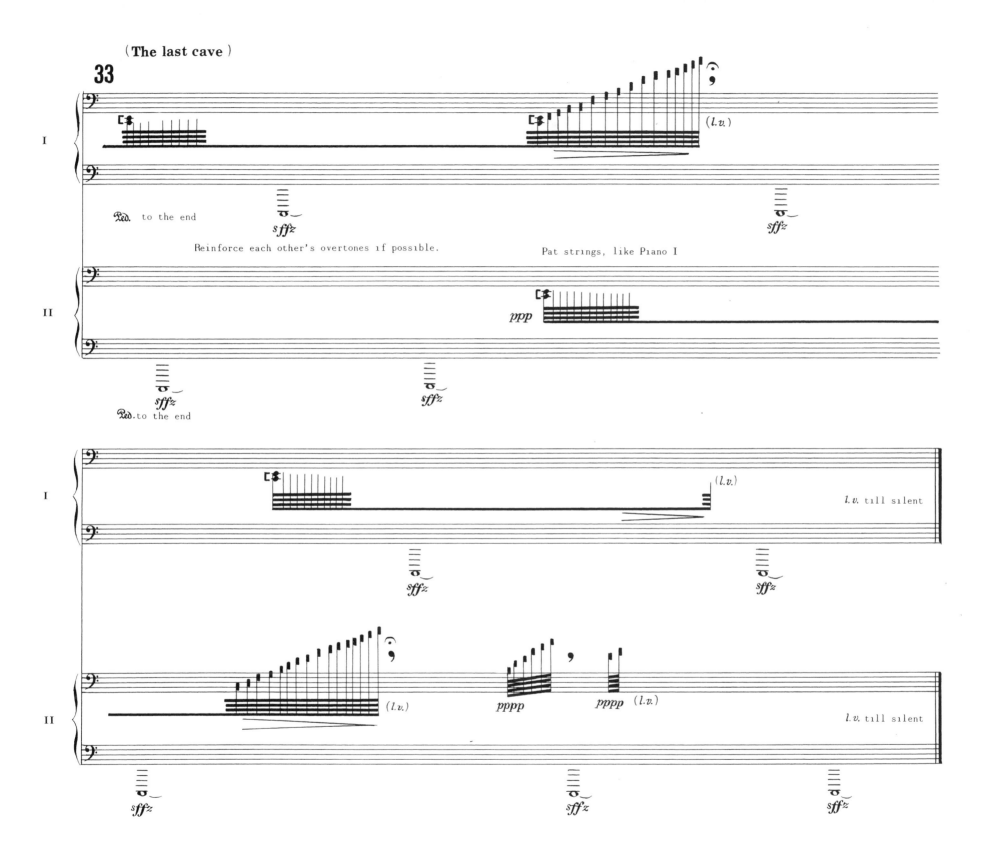

The fresco painters had to work quickly before the plaster dried. I am sure that the only good thing the American bombers did, and inadvertently, in World War II, was to uncover the rough sketches (*sinopie*) underneath the fresco paintings. The force of the bombs they dropped made the first layer of plaster fall and left the sketches bare, so that we would know the secrets of the great fresco masters. They might practice, almost like instrumental performers, on sketch paper beforehand; but when the actual painting was to be be realized, they had to work quickly. This undoubtedly contributed to the energy and size of their work.

I have tried to work as quickly as I could, hoping that the forethought, as in the case of the fresco painters, would lie behind, and not before, the next note. These FRESCOES are written or painted with a wide brush, and must be played with the same energy and abandon they were written in.

Placement of Players and Instruments

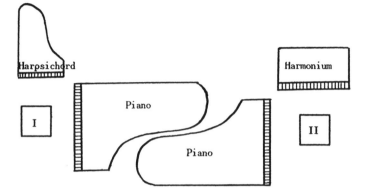

It probably would be best to have the tops off the pianos. The harpsichord should be a large one if possible, but one can put a microphone into a smaller one and that will do. Do not use an electric harpsichord. The dynamic indications are only to indicate style of playing and I don't expect them to be attempted for their usual meaning.

The harmonium, also not an electric organ, should be an electrified parlor organ of the reed variety (generally the Estey models of around 1910 are about the best). It can be a pump organ but this will make a lot of work for the second pianist. Care must be taken to find an instrument that does not make too much blower noise.

Glossary

———→ = accel.   ←——— = rit.

𝅘𝅥𝅮𝅘𝅥𝅮𝅘𝅥𝅮 = free-time, not-too-fast grace notes

𝅘𝅥𝅮𝅘𝅥𝅮𝅘𝅥𝅮 = play unevenly: That is, with unequal duration of notes

𝅘𝅥𝅮𝅘𝅥𝅮𝅘𝅥𝅮 = accel.   𝅘𝅥𝅮𝅘𝅥𝅮𝅘𝅥𝅮 = rit.

↓ = cue from player to player; ↕ = general cue   In free measures, notes placed vertically do not necessarily coincide (unless there is an implied pulse) if there is no cue-arrow

𝄾 𝄾 𝄾 𝄾 𝄾 long to short commas (5" - 1/4" approx.)

𝄙𝄙𝄙𝄙 repeat or extend figure the length of the beam.

⌣ = above note, pluck with nail   ↧ = pluck or strike with flesh of finger

⌀ = free time signature

〜〜〜✲ flutter pedal

⊏ indicates a tone cluster

In free time, accidentals are retained throughout and in beamed groups.
In metered time accidentals follow usual practice. Where proportional notation dictates long beams, accidentals apply only to the note they precede.

WILLIAM BOLCOM
May 1971